LEGO® MODELERS

BUILD FABULOUS
FIGURES

ILLUSTRATED BY SEBASTIAN QUIGLEY

DK Publishing, Inc.

BALLERINA

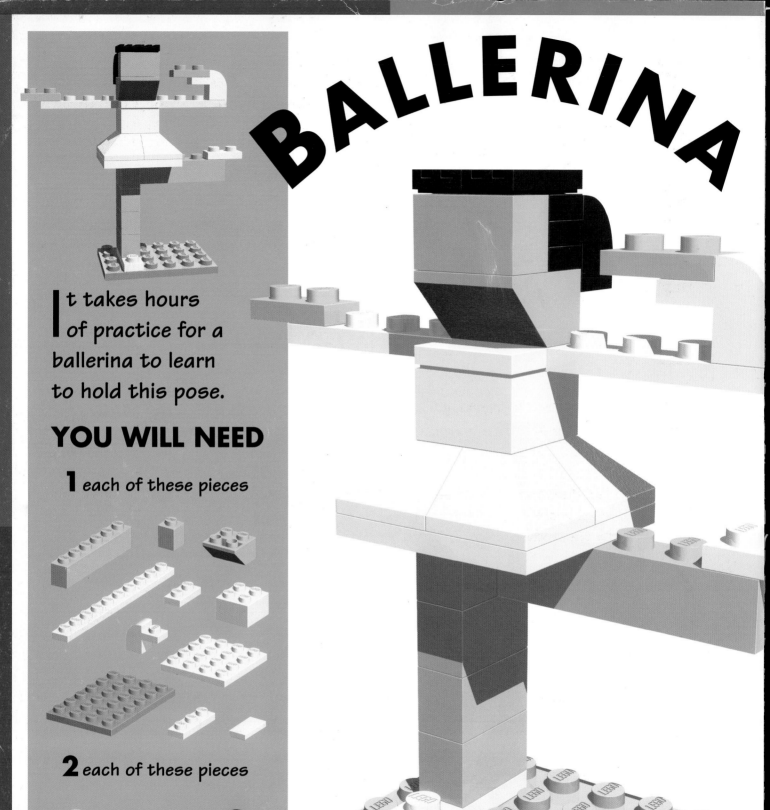

It takes hours of practice for a ballerina to learn to hold this pose.

YOU WILL NEED

1 each of these pieces

2 each of these pieces

4 each of these pieces

This beautiful ballerina is now ready to practice her pirouettes!

There are **27** bricks in this ballerina model.

6

5

4

These bricks will make her hair.

3

2

1

START with the ballerina's head.

IDEAS
• Change the color of the ballerina's tutu — she'll need a new costume for every ballet she dances.
• Make two horizontal legs for the ballerina — then she will do the splits!

8

Attach the head to the body.

7

6

5

Now build her legs. Remember to attach the two white ballet shoes.

4

3

Add these two yellow bricks for the hands.

4

3

2

2

1

BUILD this model from the base brick upward.

1

Now make the ballerina's body — don't forget her tutu!

BODY BUILDER

This big bodybuilder will be one of your strongest models!

YOU WILL NEED

1 each of these pieces

2 each of these pieces

4 of this piece

There are **32** bricks in this bodybuilder model.

8

7

Now give your model some hair.

6

5

Remember to attach these bricks! The arms will fit on later.

4

3

2

1

START with the body and carefully build in layers.

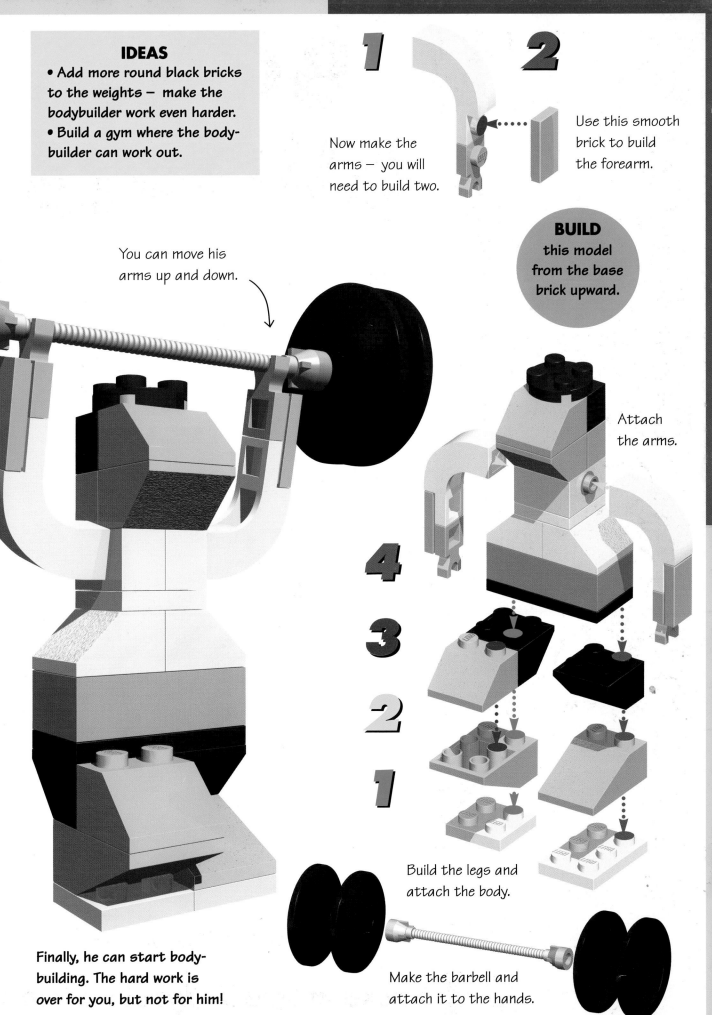

1 Now make the arms — you will need to build two.

2 Use this smooth brick to build the forearm.

You can move his arms up and down.

BUILD this model from the base brick upward.

Attach the arms.

4

3

2

1 Build the legs and attach the body.

Finally, he can start body-building. The hard work is over for you, but not for him!

Make the barbell and attach it to the hands.

ROLLER SKATER

T his roller skater is learning to balance on his skates, but he's still a bit wobbly.

BUILD this model from the base brick upward.

If you don't have these bricks for the eyes, use plain bricks instead.

Follow each step carefully.

9
8
7
6
5
4
3
2
1

START with the roller skater's body.

1 each of these pieces

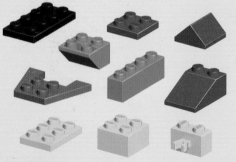

2 each of these pieces

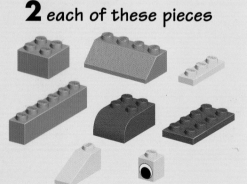

4 each of these pieces

There are **34** bricks in this roller skater model.

5

4

3

2

1

Next, build the legs and the roller skates. Remember to make two.

IDEAS
• Change the wheels on the roller skates to single thin bricks. Then your model can go ice-skating instead!

Your roller skater model will soon be whizzing around to see all his friends!

6

5

Finally attach the legs and arms to the body.

SOCCER PLAYER

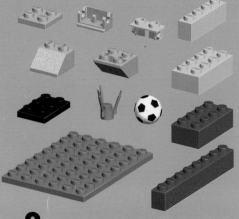

This soccer player dazzles his fans with his fancy footwork on the football field.

YOU WILL NEED

1 each of these pieces

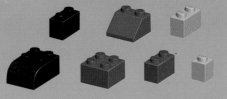

2 each of these pieces

8 of this piece

8

7 This is the face. You could use "eye" bricks if you have them!

6

BUILD this model from the base brick upward.

5

4 The arms will attach to this brick later.

3

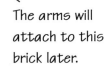

2

1 START with the player's body.

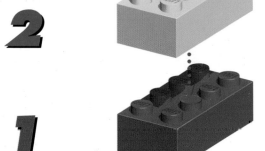

There are **35** bricks in this soccer player model.

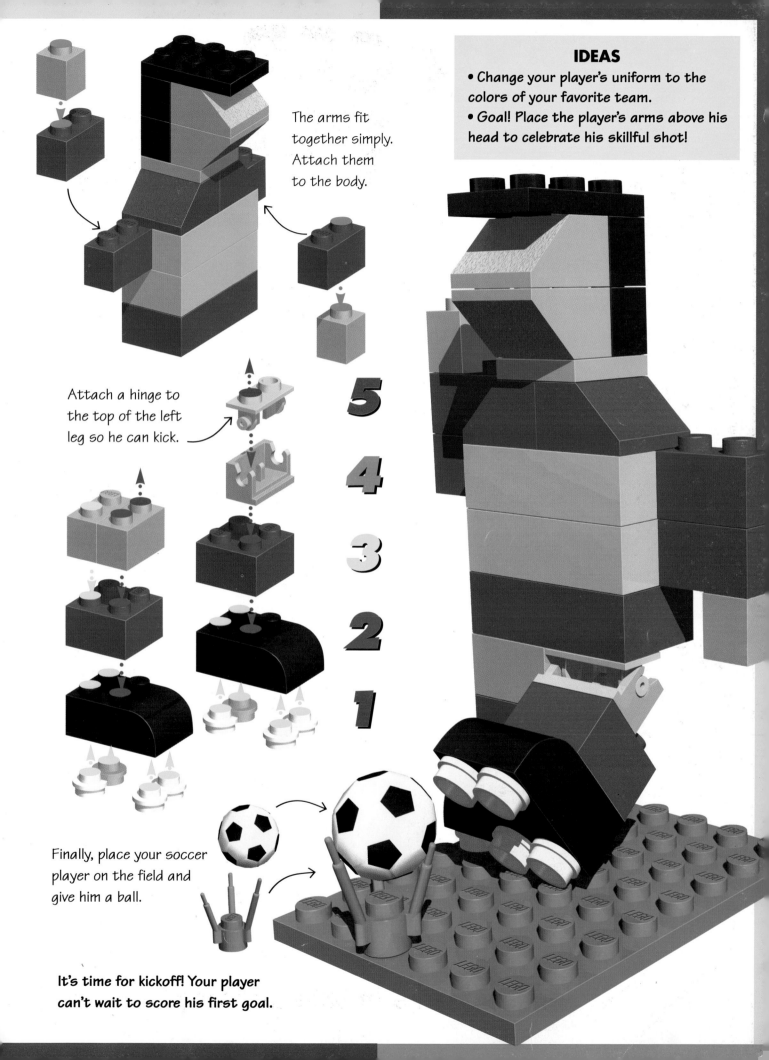

The arms fit together simply. Attach them to the body.

IDEAS
• Change your player's uniform to the colors of your favorite team.
• Goal! Place the player's arms above his head to celebrate his skillful shot!

Attach a hinge to the top of the left leg so he can kick.

5
4
3
2
1

Finally, place your soccer player on the field and give him a ball.

It's time for kickoff! Your player can't wait to score his first goal.

GOLFER

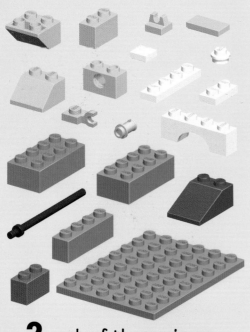

T his golfer swings his club, hoping to score a hole in one.

YOU WILL NEED

1 each of these pieces

2 each of these pieces

4 of this piece

BUILD
this model from the base brick upward.

Now build the shoulders and the head.

Don't forget to add these two bricks. The golf club will attach here later.

START with the golfer's body.

9

8

7

6

5

4

3

2

1

There are **36** bricks in this golfer model.

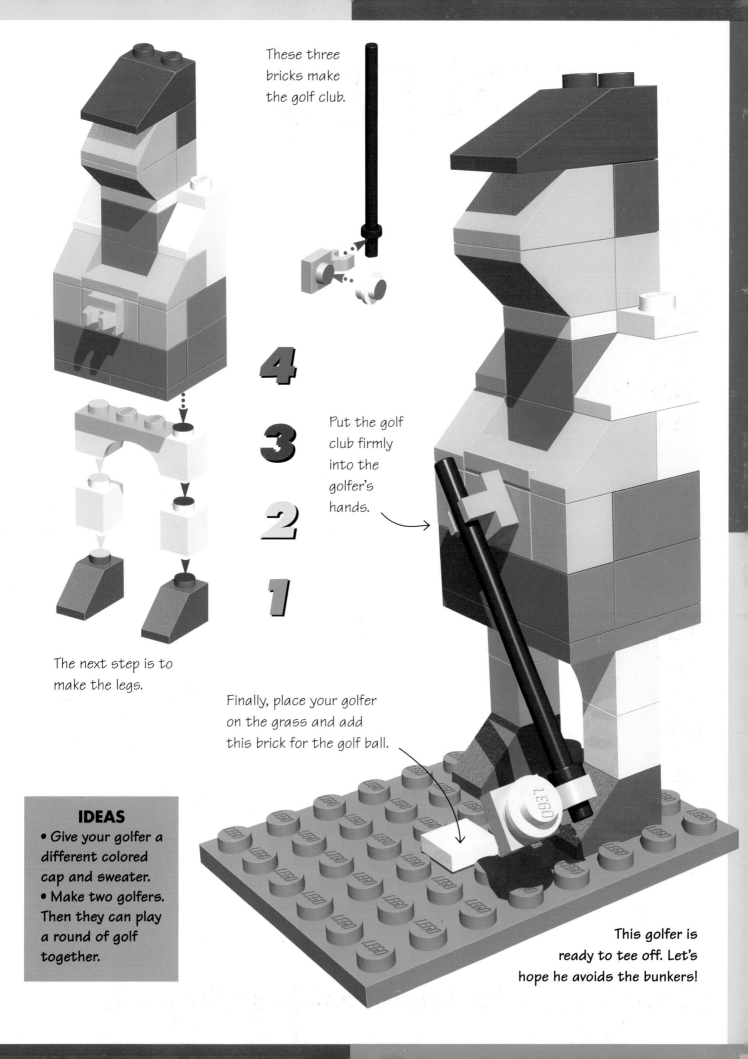

These three bricks make the golf club.

4

3

2

1

The next step is to make the legs.

Put the golf club firmly into the golfer's hands.

Finally, place your golfer on the grass and add this brick for the golf ball.

IDEAS
• Give your golfer a different colored cap and sweater.
• Make two golfers. Then they can play a round of golf together.

This golfer is ready to tee off. Let's hope he avoids the bunkers!

SKATEBOARDER

Watch this skateboarder zip past! He is the fastest kid in town!

YOU WILL NEED

1 each of these pieces

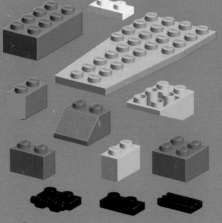

2 each of these pieces

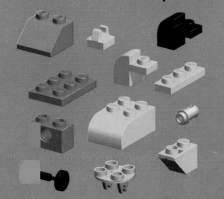

BUILD this model from the base brick upward.

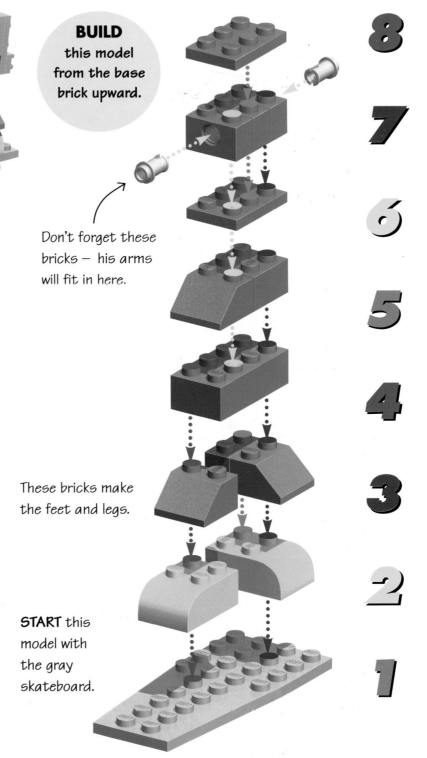

Don't forget these bricks — his arms will fit in here.

These bricks make the feet and legs.

START this model with the gray skateboard.

8

7

6

5

4

3

2

1

There are **36** bricks in this skateboarder model.

Now make two arms. Follow the arrows!

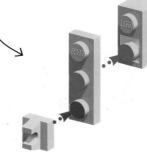

7
6
5
4
3
2
1

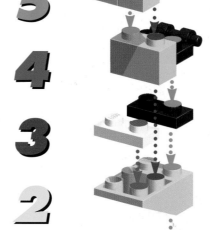

Now build the head onto the body.

Attach the two arms.

Finally, attach the wheels underneath the skateboard.

Your skateboarder is ready to roll — how many tricks can he do?

DRUMMER

Y ou can't miss this drummer when he marches down the street, banging his cymbal and drum.

YOU WILL NEED

1 each of these pieces

2 each of these pieces

Now build the drum and cymbal.

These bricks make the right arm.

This brick is hidden here. The arm will attach here later.

BUILD this model from the base brick upward.

START with the drummer's body.

There are **39** bricks in this drummer model.

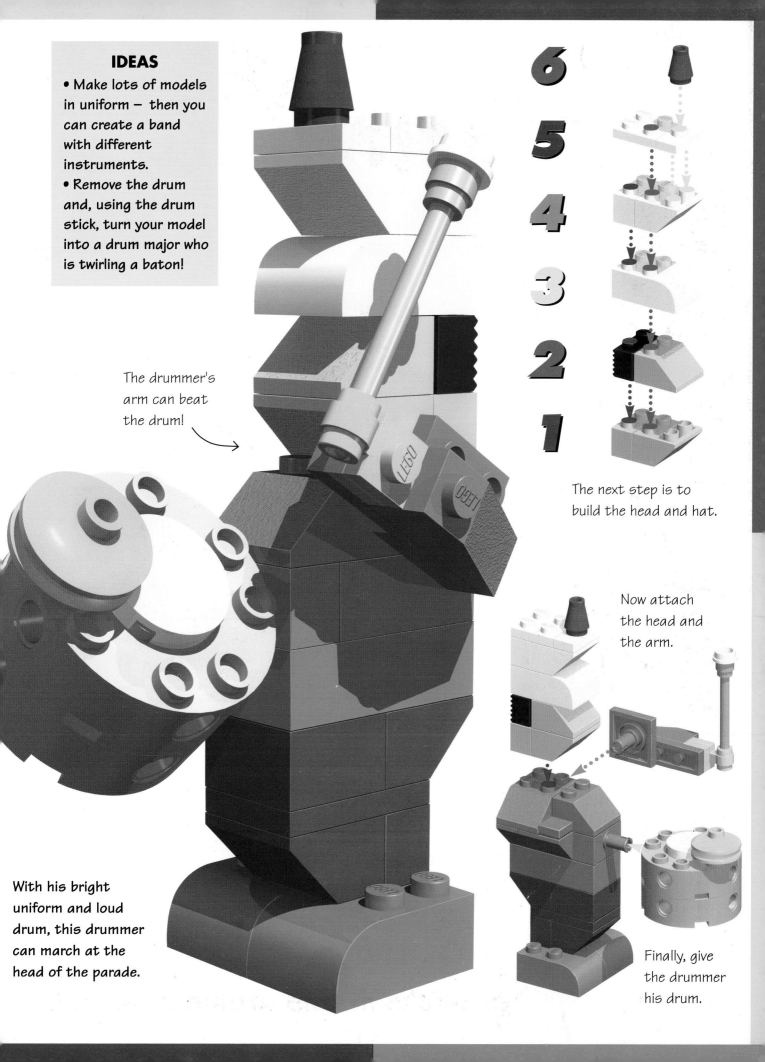

The drummer's arm can beat the drum!

6
5
4
3
2
1

The next step is to build the head and hat.

Now attach the head and the arm.

With his bright uniform and loud drum, this drummer can march at the head of the parade.

Finally, give the drummer his drum.

CAMERAMAN

This cameraman loves to capture his friends on video!

YOU WILL NEED

1 each of these pieces

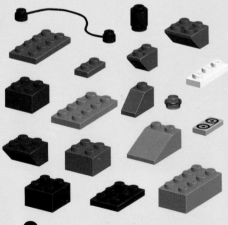

2 each of these pieces

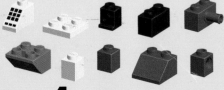

4 of this piece

There are **42** bricks in this cameraman model.

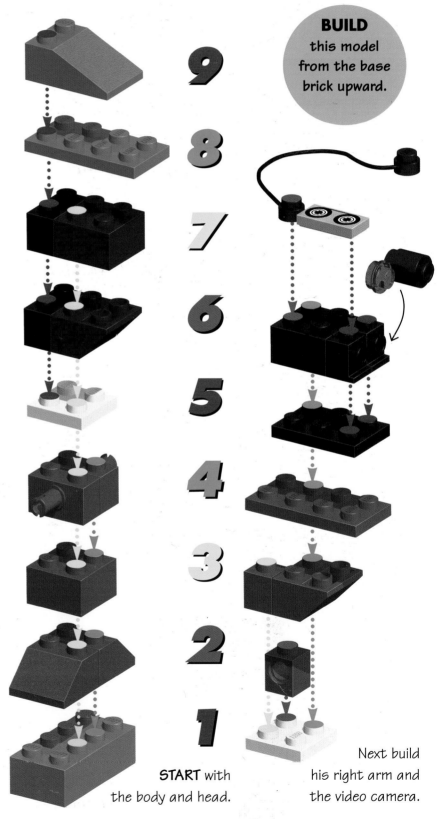

BUILD this model from the base brick upward.

9

8

7

6

5

4

3

2

1

START with the body and head.

Next build his right arm and the video camera.

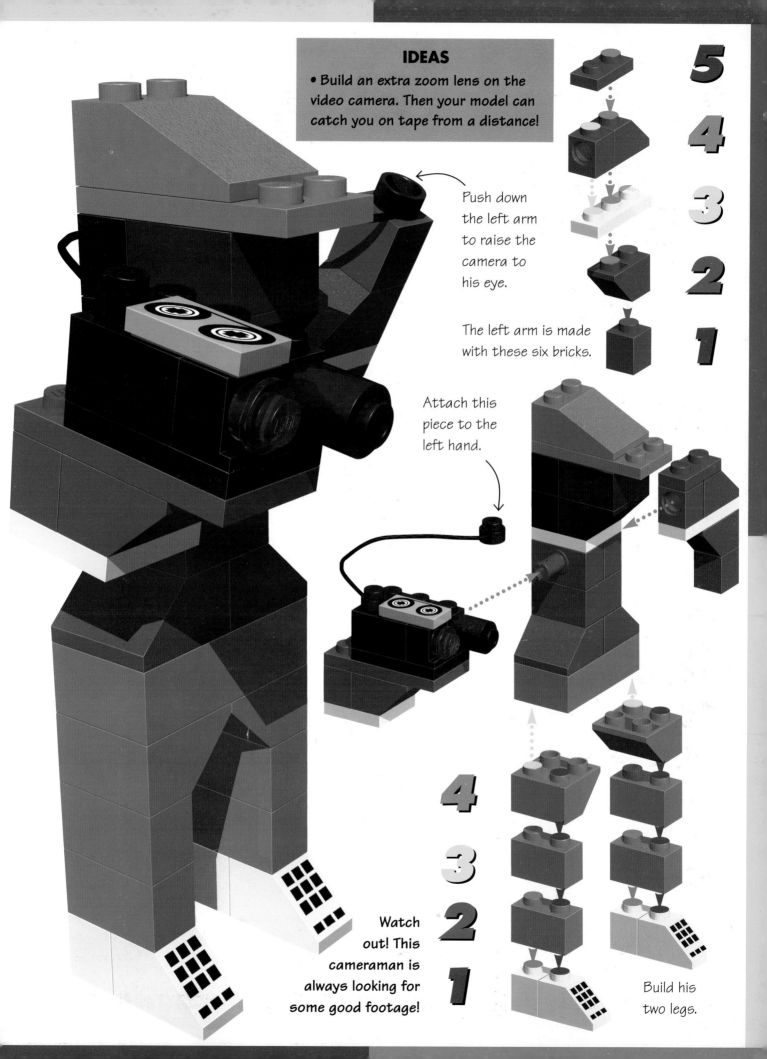

**5
4
3
2
1**

IDEAS
• Build an extra zoom lens on the video camera. Then your model can catch you on tape from a distance!

Push down the left arm to raise the camera to his eye.

The left arm is made with these six bricks.

Attach this piece to the left hand.

**4
3
2
1**

Watch out! This cameraman is always looking for some good footage!

Build his two legs.

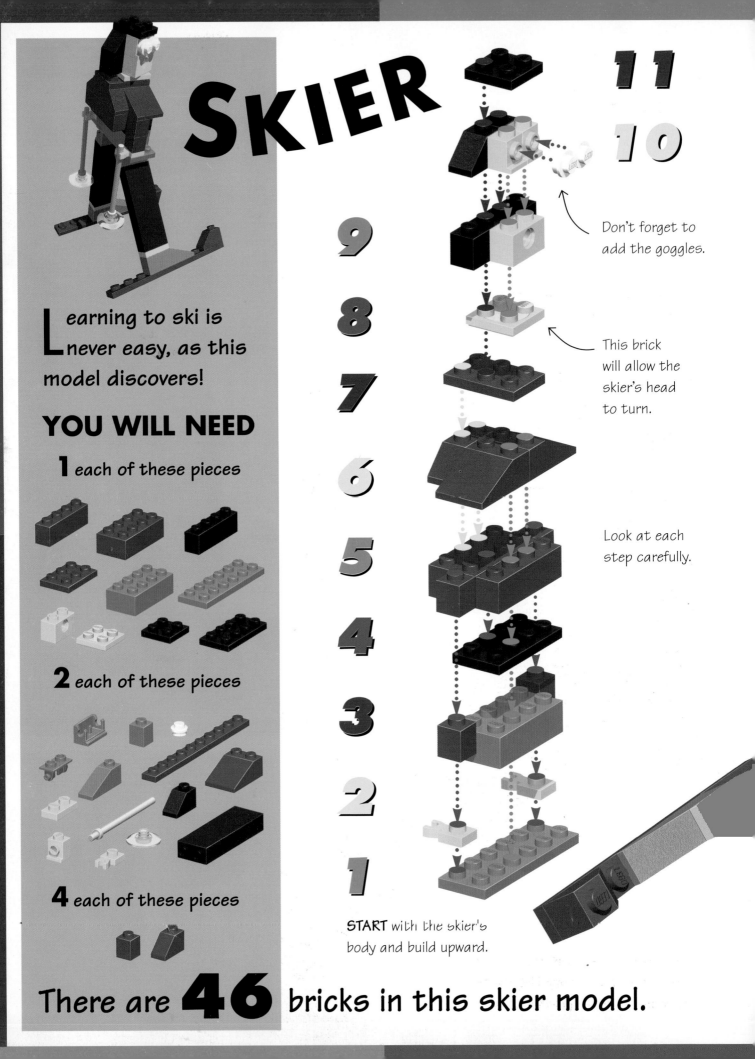

SKIER

11

10

Don't forget to add the goggles.

9

8

This brick will allow the skier's head to turn.

7

6

Look at each step carefully.

5

4

3

2

1

START with the skier's body and build upward.

L earning to ski is never easy, as this model discovers!

YOU WILL NEED

1 each of these pieces

2 each of these pieces

4 each of these pieces

There are **46** bricks in this skier model.

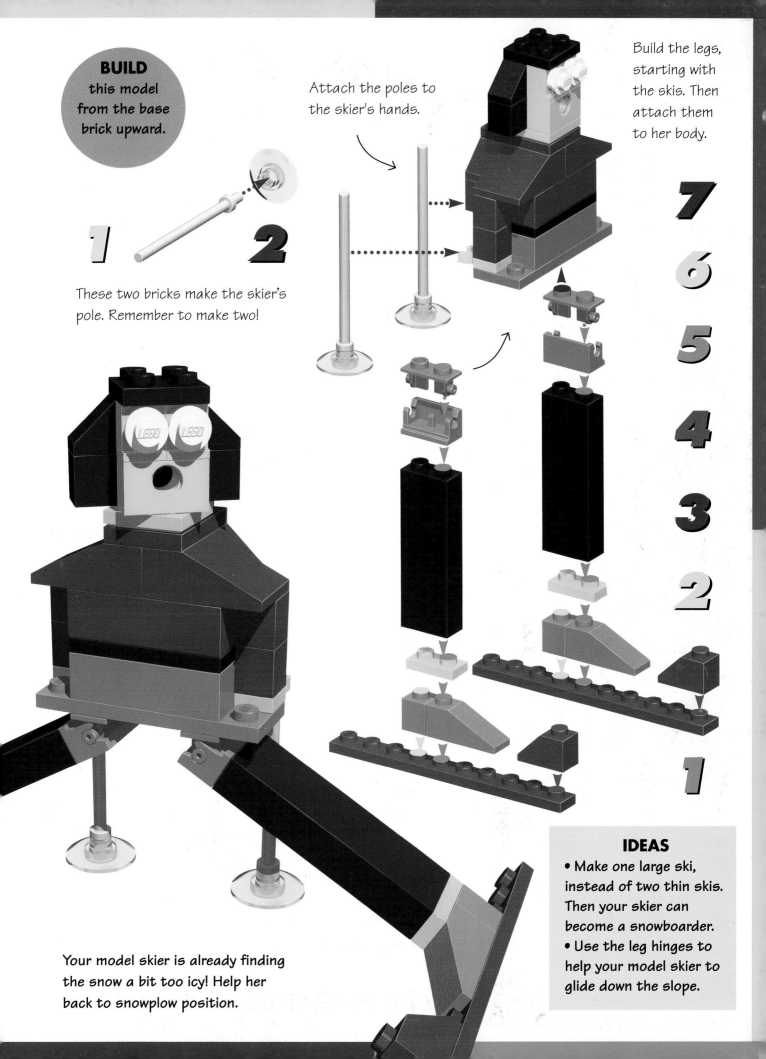

BUILD this model from the base brick upward.

1

These two bricks make the skier's pole. Remember to make two!

2

Attach the poles to the skier's hands.

Build the legs, starting with the skis. Then attach them to her body.

7
6
5
4
3
2
1

Your model skier is already finding the snow a bit too icy! Help her back to snowplow position.

IDEAS
• Make one large ski, instead of two thin skis. Then your skier can become a snowboarder.
• Use the leg hinges to help your model skier to glide down the slope.

BASEBALL

With one swing, the baseball goes flying – this player sure can hit hard!

YOU WILL NEED

1 each of these pieces

2 each of these pieces

3 each of these pieces

6 of this piece

8 of this piece

There are **50** bricks in this baseball player model.

BUILD this model from the base brick upward.

This brick will enable the baseball player's head to turn. If you do not have this brick, use a plain yellow brick instead.

Look carefully at each step before placing your bricks.

START with the baseball player's body.

10

9

8

7

6

5

4

3

2

1

PLAYER

The next step is to make the bat.

Now attach the bat onto the hand as shown.

Finally, place the legs onto the small patch of grass.

6
5
4
3
2
1

Batter up! This baseball player is ready to hit another home run.

IDEAS
• Make two teams of baseball players and a baseball diamond on which to play.

ARTIST

T his artist loves creating pictures with her palette of colorful paints.

YOU WILL NEED

1 each of these pieces

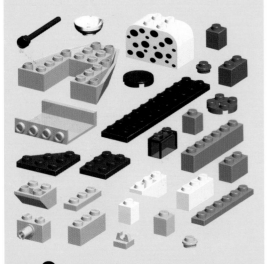

2 each of these pieces

3 each of these pieces

There are **54** bricks in this artist model.

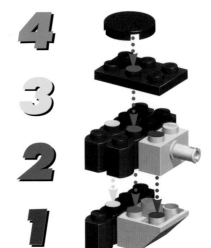

4
3
2
1

START with the head.

IDEAS
• Create your own painting on the easel. There are so many things this artist can draw!
• Change the artist's clothes – it is easy to spill paint on overalls!

7
6
5
4
3
2
1

Now build the artist's body.

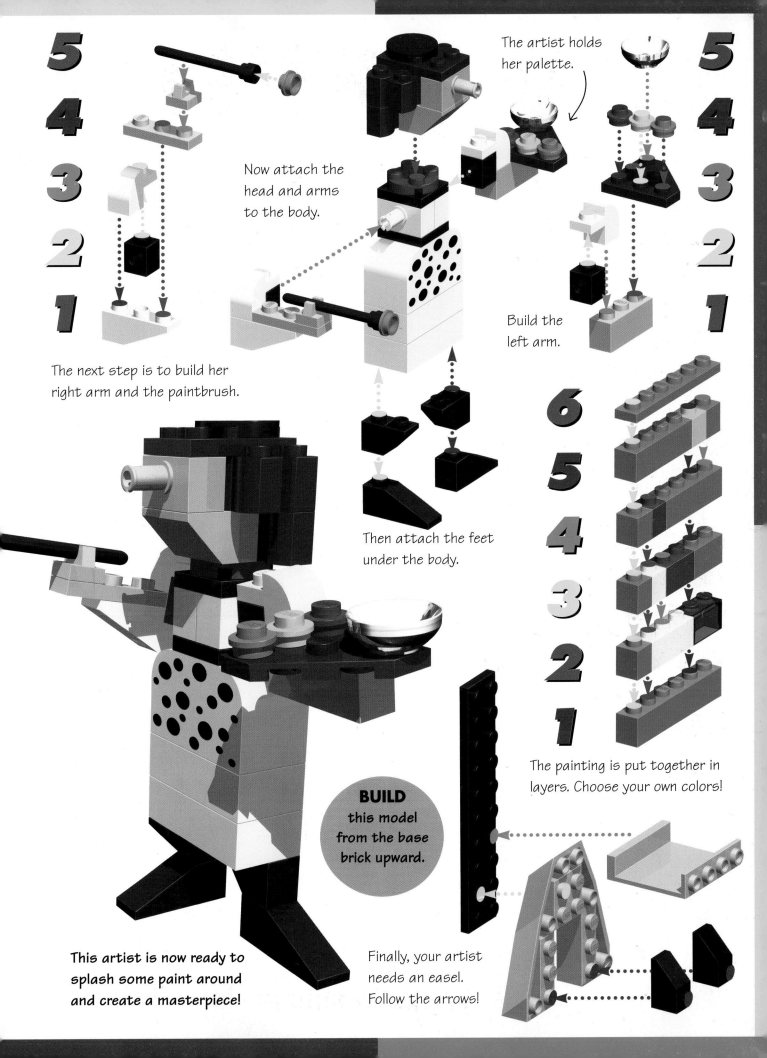

5
4
3
2
1

The next step is to build her right arm and the paintbrush.

Now attach the head and arms to the body.

The artist holds her palette.

5
4
3
2
1

Build the left arm.

Then attach the feet under the body.

6
5
4
3
2
1

The painting is put together in layers. Choose your own colors!

BUILD this model from the base brick upward.

This artist is now ready to splash some paint around and create a masterpiece!

Finally, your artist needs an easel. Follow the arrows!

BREAK DANCER

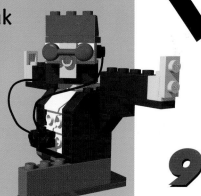

This break dancer just loves to show off his moves to his friends!

YOU WILL NEED

1 each of these pieces

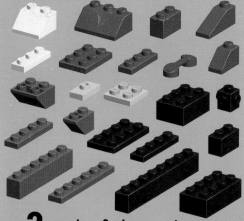

2 each of these pieces

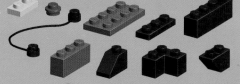

3 of this piece

4 of this piece

7 of this piece

There are **57** bricks in this break dancer model.

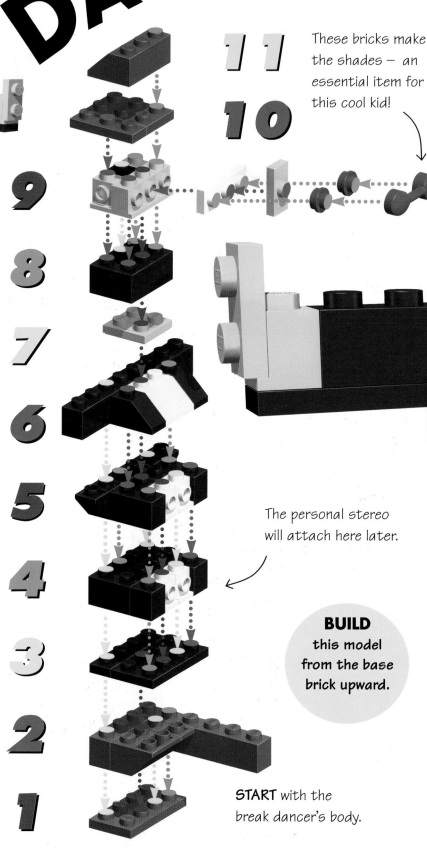

11

10

These bricks make the shades — an essential item for this cool kid!

9

8

7

6

5

4

The personal stereo will attach here later.

BUILD this model from the base brick upward.

3

2

1

START with the break dancer's body.

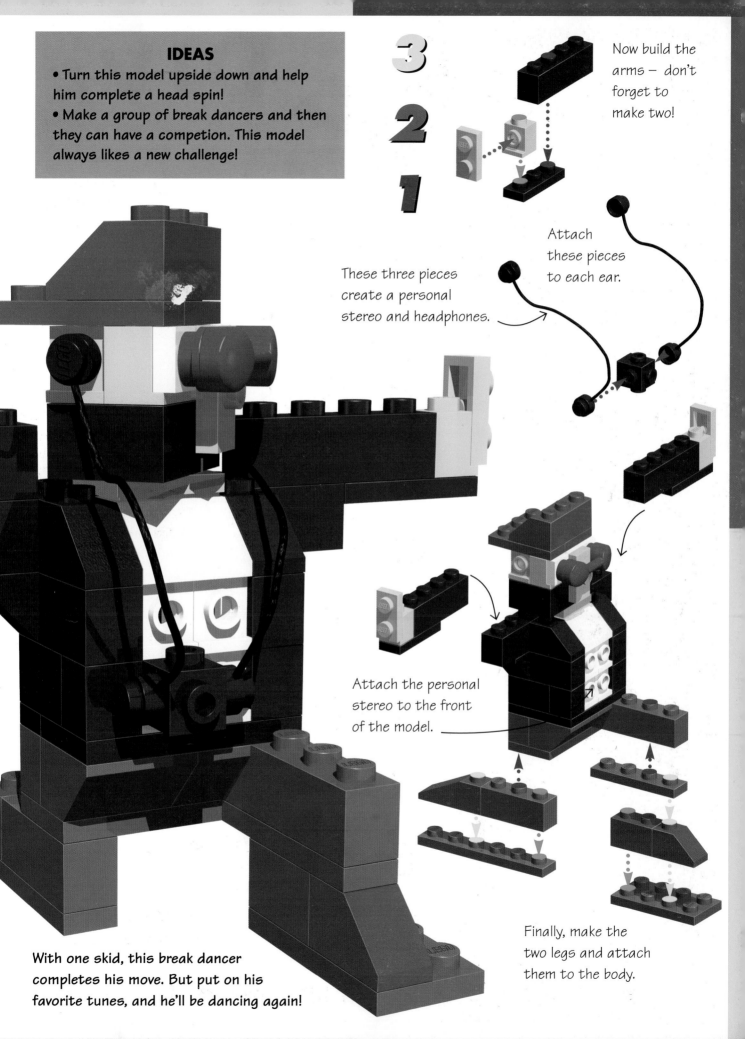

3
2
1

Now build the arms – don't forget to make two!

Attach these pieces to each ear.

These three pieces create a personal stereo and headphones.

Attach the personal stereo to the front of the model.

Finally, make the two legs and attach them to the body.

With one skid, this break dancer completes his move. But put on his favorite tunes, and he'll be dancing again!

SCUBA DIVER

This diver likes to explore the depths of the ocean.

YOU WILL NEED

1 each of these pieces

2 each of these pieces

3 each of these pieces

4 each of these pieces

5 of this piece

There are **57** bricks in this scuba diver model.

9

8

Follow the black arrows to attach this tube.

7

This brick will be the diver's mask.

6

Make the diver's breathing apparatus.

5

BUILD this model from the base brick upward.

4

3

2

1

START with the diver's body.

3

2

1

These bricks will create the oxygen tanks. Make two of these.

Make two of these arms — they will fit onto the body later.

Attach the two cylinders under the blue brick.

Now attach the two arms.

6

5

Finally make the legs. Don't forget the flippers!

4

3

2

1

At last! Now your diver can plunge into deep waters to see the coral reefs.

IDEAS

• Build an underwater world with sharks and fish for your diver to find!

• Remove the diver's mask and tanks and give him a board — he will become a bodyboarder looking for the perfect wave!

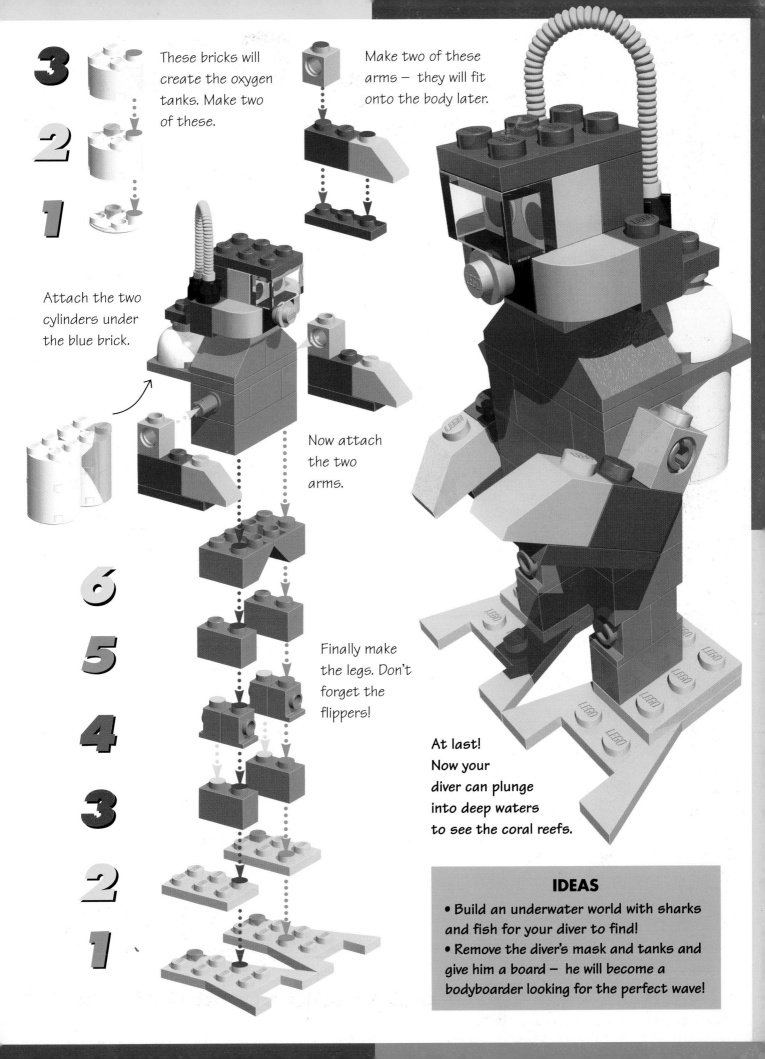

See if you can build this guitarist. He is crazy about his music!

YOU WILL NEED

1 each of these pieces

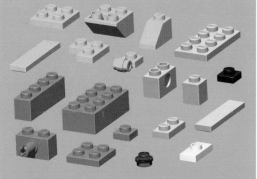

2 each of these pieces

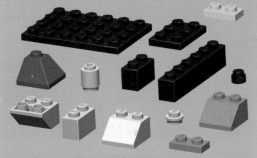

3 of this piece

4 each of these pieces

8 of this piece

ROCK STAR

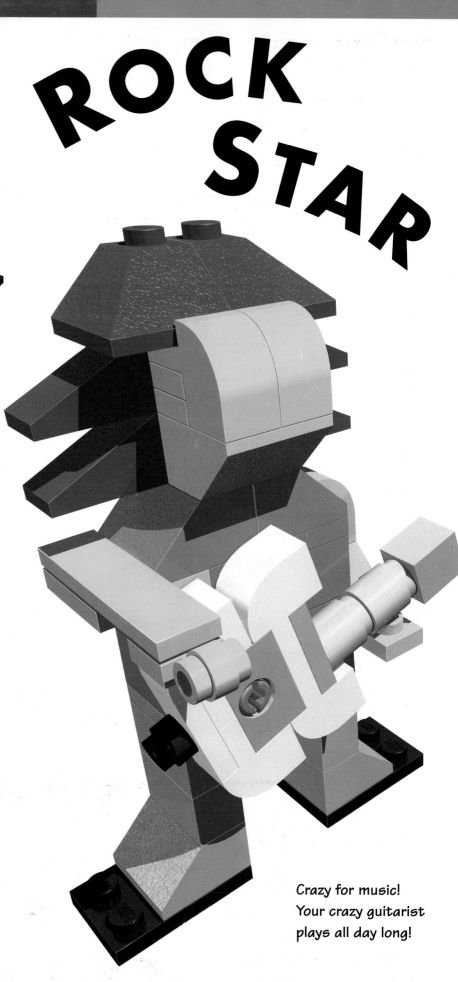

Crazy for music! Your crazy guitarist plays all day long!

There are **66** bricks in this rock star model.

Now it is time to add that wild mop of red hair!

7

6

5

4

3

2

1

START with the rock star's body.

8

These five pieces make up the face. Attach this in front of the red hair.

BUILD this model from the base brick upward.

Attach the guitar to his body as shown.

Now make the guitar. Start with the base brick.

Don't forget to add the fringe – use these two sloping bricks.

The legs are easy to make. Build two the same.

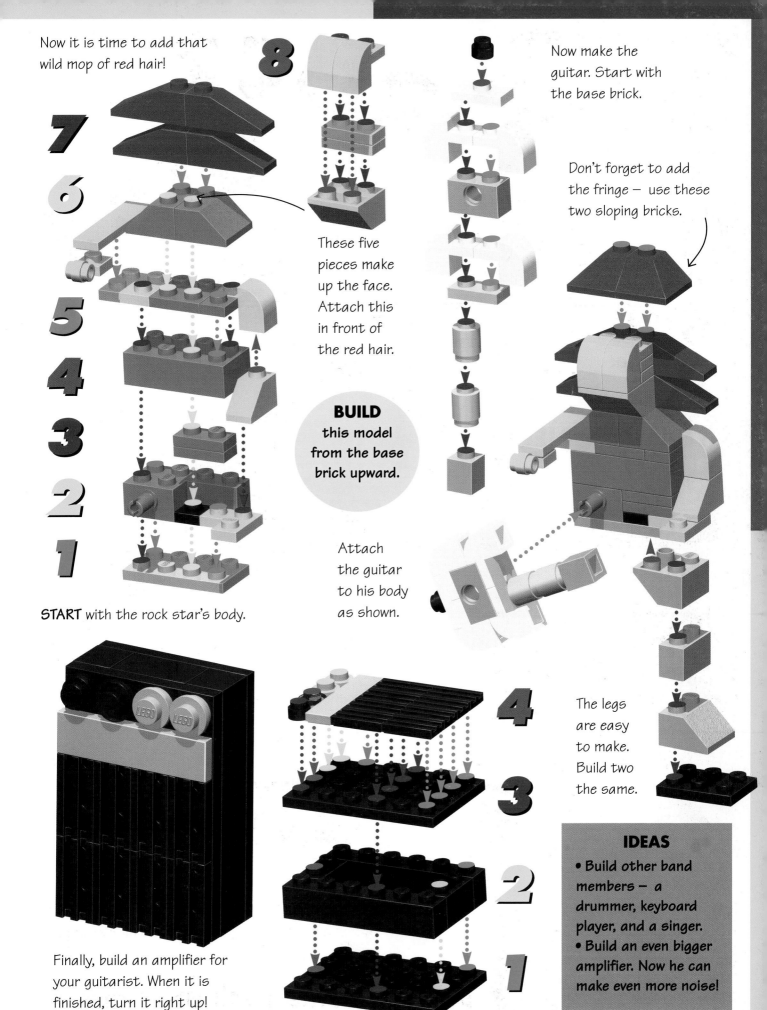

4

3

2

1

Finally, build an amplifier for your guitarist. When it is finished, turn it right up!

IDEAS
• Build other band members – a drummer, keyboard player, and a singer.
• Build an even bigger amplifier. Now he can make even more noise!

GOALKEEPER

This ice hockey goalkeeper has to stay alert to stop the fast pucks.

YOU WILL NEED

1 each of these pieces

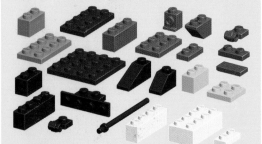

2 each of these pieces

3 each of these pieces

4 of this piece

7 of this piece

There are **71** bricks in this goalkeeper model.

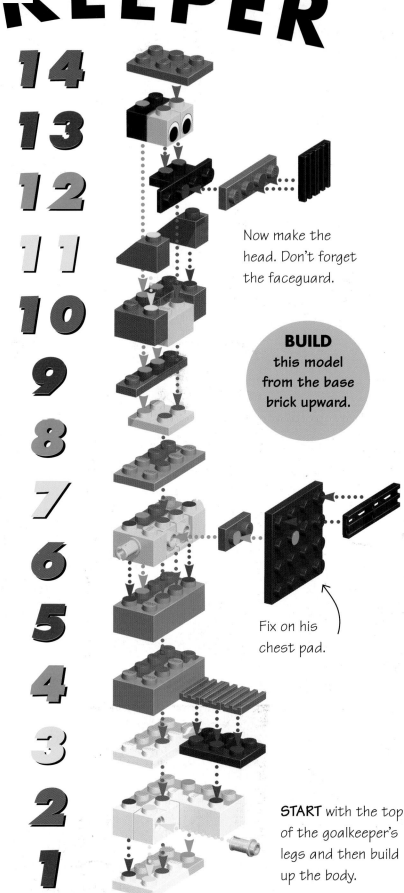

Now make the head. Don't forget the faceguard.

BUILD this model from the base brick upward.

Fix on his chest pad.

START with the top of the goalkeeper's legs and then build up the body.

The next
step is
to build
his arms.

4

3

2

1

5

Join the two
arms to the
body, as shown.

Remember to add
the shin pads!

6

Give your goalkeeper
his hockey stick.

7

These bricks
make the
lower legs.

IDEAS
• Build a goal. Then
your model can
practice his saves.

The hockey
stick fits
together
simply.

With all his padding on, this model
is ready to stop the whizzing puck!

To find out how you can purchase LEGO toys on-line visit:

www.legoworldshop.com

THE LEGO BOOK RANGE ALSO INCLUDES:

LEGO MODELERS:	**ROAD MAZE GAME BOOKS:**
Build Amazing Animals	Spy Catcher
	Jewel Thief
PUZZLE STORYBOOKS:	Treasure Smuggler
The Lost Temple	Gold Robber
Rock Raiders	
Castle Mystery	**ALSO LOOK FOR:**
The Curse of the Mummy	The Ultimate LEGO Book

A DK PUBLISHING BOOK
www.dk.com

Text copyright © 1999 LEGO Group
Illustrations © 1999 LEGO Group
Art Editor: Goldberry Broad
Project Editor: Rebecca Smith
Managing Art Editor: Cathy Tincknell
Managing Editor: Joanna Devereux
DTP Designer: Jill Bunyan
Production: Steve Lang

First American Edition, 1999
2 4 6 8 10 9 7 5 3 1

Published in the United States by
DK Publishing, Inc.
95 Madison Avenue
New York, New York 10016

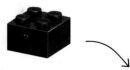

A CIP catalog record for this book is available from the Library of Congress.

ISBN 0-7894-4777-0

Color reproduction by Media Development
Printed and bound in Italy by L.E.G.O.

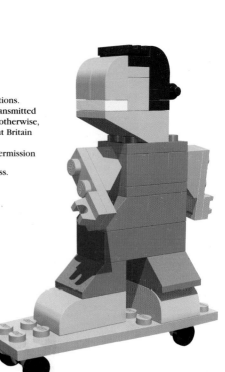